D1007658

SPECIAL EDITION

THE OPEN MEDIA PAMPHLET SERIES

OTHER TITLES IN THE OPEN MEDIA PAMPHLET SERIES

The Case of Mumia Abu-Jamal

A Life in the Balance

AMNESTY INTERNATIONAL

Open Media Pamphlet Series editor Greg Ruggiero

SEVEN STORIES PRESS / New York

ISBN 1-58322-081-X

Book design by Cindy LaBreacht
9 8 7 6 5 4 3 2 1
Printed in Canada.

Mumia Abu-Jamal has been incarcerated on Pennsylvania's death row for the past 17 years. His case has generated more controversy and received more attention, both national and international, than that of any other inmate currently under sentence of death in the United States of America (USA).

Mumia Abu-Jamal, black, was convicted and sentenced to death in July 1982 for the murder of white police officer Daniel Faulkner on 9 December 1981. He has steadfastly maintained his innocence since 1981. Since the trial, those advocating his release or retrial have contested the validity of much of the evidence used to obtain his conviction. These accusations have been countered by members of the law enforcement community and their supporters, who have agitated for Mumia Abu-Jamal's execution while maintaining that the trial was unbiased and fair.

In light of the contradictory and incomplete evidence in this case, Amnesty International can take no position on the guilt or innocence of Mumia Abu-Jamal. Nor has the organization identified him as a political prisoner, although it has previously expressed its concern over the activities of a government counterintelligence program, which appeared to number Abu-Jamal among its targets (see page 24). However, the organization is concerned that political statements attributed to him as a teenager were improperly used by the prosecution in its efforts to obtain a death sentence against him. In any event, the administration of the death penalty in the USA remains a highly politicized affair, sanctioned and supported by elected officials for its perceived political advantages. The politicization of Mumia Abu-Jamal's case may not only have prejudiced his right to a fair trial, but may now be undermining his right to fair and impartial treatment in the appeal courts.

After many years of monitoring Mumia Abu-Jamal's case and a thorough study of original documents, including the entire trial transcript, the organization has concluded that the proceedings used to convict and sentence Mumia Abu-Jamal to death were in violation of minimum international standards that govern fair trial procedures and the use of the death penalty. Amnesty International therefore believes that the interests of justice would best be served by the granting of a new trial to Mumia Abu-Jamal (see conclusion).

In October 1999, Abu-Jamal filed his initial federal appeal. The federal courts represent Abu-Jamal's final opportunity to have many of the troubling issues in his case addressed and corrected. However, as discussed below, the 1996 *Anti-terrorism and Effective Death Penalty Act* severely limits the federal courts' ability to ensure that legal proceedings at state-level guaranteed the defendants' rights enshrined in the US Constitution and under international human rights standards. Amnesty International has chosen this time, a time when Abu-Jamal's life is in the balance, to release this report.

Mumia Abu-Jamal is one of more than three and a half thousand people on death row in 37 states and under federal law throughout the USA. By the end of 1999, 598 prisoners had been put to death in 30 states since executions resumed in 1977; in 1999 alone, 98 prisoners died at the hands of the state, a record year since the 1950s. The US authorities have repeatedly violated international minimum safeguards in their continuing resort to capital punishment. Violations include the execution of the mentally impaired, of child offenders, and of those who received inadequate legal representation at trial. Those sentenced to death in the USA are overwhelmingly the poor, and disproportionately come from racial and ethnic minority communities. The risk of wrongful conviction remains high, with more than 80 prisoners released from death rows since 1973 after evidence of their innocence emerged. Many came close to execution before the courts acted on their claims of wrongful conviction. Others have gone to their deaths despite serious doubts concerning their guilt.

Amnesty International unconditionally opposes the death penalty under all circumstances. Even if it were possible for a country to create a judicial system entirely fair and free from bias and error, the punishment of death would still violate the most fundamental of all human rights. Each death sentence and execution is an affront to human dignity: the ultimate form of cruel, inhuman and degrading punishment.

In opposing the death penalty, Amnesty International in no way seeks to minimize or condone the crimes for which those sentenced to death and executed were convicted. Nor does the organization seek to belittle the appalling suffering of the families of murder victims, for whom it has the greatest sympathy. However, the finality and cruelty inherent in the death penalty render it incompatible with norms of modern day civilized behaviour and an inappropriate and unacceptable response to violent crime.

The continued and accelerating use of the death penalty is one of many serious human rights violations that Amnesty International has identified and repeatedly raised with the US authorities. These other concerns include a nationwide pattern of police brutality; the physical and sexual abuse of prisoners, inhuman or degrading conditions of confinement and the mistreatment of asylum seekers.[1]

THE BACKDROP: PHILADELPHIA, A CITY OF RACIAL TENSIONS, POLICE BRUTALITY AND POLICE CORRUPTION

The shooting of Officer Daniel Faulkner in 1981 and Mumia Abu-Jamal's trial the following year took place in Philadelphia, a city fraught with tension between the predominately white authorities and the African American and other minority communities. Both before and since that time, numerous instances have come to light of police brutality and the use of disproportionate force with lethal consequences; of the corruption of police officers and the fabrication of evidence against those suspected of criminal acts.[2]

In 1973, a federal judge for the US District Court stated that police abuse occurred with such frequency in Philadelphia that it could not be "dismissed as rare, isolated instances" and that city officials did "little or nothing" to punish or prevent police abuse.

In 1979, the US Department of Justice filed a lawsuit against the then-mayor of Philadelphia, Frank Rizzo, and other city officials for condoning police brutality. The lawsuit listed 290 persons shot by the city's police officers between 1975 and 1979, the majority of whom were from ethnic minorities. During Frank Rizzo's eight years as mayor, fatal shootings by Philadelphia police officers increased by 20 per cent annually. In the year after he left office, 1980, fatal shootings declined 67 per cent.[3] Mayor Rizzo appeared to tolerate police misconduct. In 1978, he told an audience of 700 police officers "Even when you're wrong, I'm going to back you."[4]

An investigation in 1978 by the Pennsylvania House of Representatives Sub-Committee on Crime and Corrections found that a small but significant number of Philadelphia police routinely engaged in verbal and physical abuse of citizens to a degree the subcommittee considered "lawless." The investigation concluded that the level of police abuse had reached that of homicidal violence and that Philadelphia lacked the necessary police leadership to control the lawlessness.

Also in 1978, the police became involved in a siege of a house occupied by members of MOVE.[5] During an attempt to force the occupants to leave the building a shot was fired, causing the police to open fire at the house (it is disputed whether the police or those in the house fired the initial shot). At this time, one police officer was fatally wounded; MOVE members later maintained that the police officer was killed by gun fire from other officers. As the occupants surrendered to the police, television cameras filmed a police officer striking Delbert Africa (all members of MOVE adopt the second name of Africa) with the butt of a shotgun and then dragging him along the ground as other police officers kicked him. Police bulldozed the house to the ground the following day, destroying the crime scene and making analysis of many of the day's events impossible.[6] Nine members of MOVE were tried on charges of third degree murder, conspiracy, and multiple counts of attempted murder and aggravated assault; all were found guilty and sentenced to 30 to 100 years in prison.

Mumia Abu-Jamal was closely involved with MOVE. It is highly likely that the officers who arrested him, although perhaps unaware of his identity, would have immediately associated him with the organization because of his dreadlocks, a hairstyle adopted by all members of MOVE as part of their beliefs. Abu-Jamal was also a former member of the Black Panther Party (BPP) and was under surveillance by the FBI's Counterintelligence Program, COINTELPRO (see box).[7] Prior to his arrest, Abu-Jamal worked as a journalist and had written articles critical of the authorities in Philadelphia. To supplement his income, he was working as a taxi cab driver at the time of the crime.

THE CRIME: THE SHOOTING OF POLICE OFFICER
DANIEL FAULKNER

On 9 December 1981, at approximately 3.55am, Officer Daniel Faulkner of the Philadelphia Police Department stopped a car driven by Mumia Abu-Jamal's brother, William Cook. A struggle ensued between the two men. Mumia Abu-Jamal, who was driving a cab in the vicinity, observed his brother in an altercation with the officer and got out of his vehicle. Minutes later, more police officers arrived on the scene to find Officer Faulkner dead from two bullet wounds to the head and back. Mumia Abu-Jamal was sitting nearby wounded in the chest by a bullet from the police officer's gun. Abu-Jamal's own legally-registered gun was found a few feet away from where he sat.

Media coverage of the case as it proceeded to trial referred extensively to Abu-Jamal's affiliations with MOVE and his former membership in the Black Panther Party. The continual references to Abu-Jamal's past political activities caused Joe Davidson, president of the Association of Black Journalists to state "[w]e are disturbed by disparaging news reports about Mr. Jamal's political and religious beliefs. As an organization dedicated to truth and fairness in journalism, we will continue to monitor media coverage on this matter. We hope that Mr. Jamal will be tried in the courtroom and not in the press."[8] Following investigations by the authorities, pre-trial hearings in the case began on 5 January 1982. On 7 June 1982, the trial of Mumia Abu-Jamal on a charge of first degree murder and possession of an instrument of crime commenced in Philadelphia, amid intense publicity.

THE TRIAL JUDGE: AN INDEPENDENT AND FAIR ARBITER OF JUSTICE?

"The judiciary shall decide matters before them impartially, on the basis of the facts and in accordance with the law, without restrictions, improper influences, inducements, pressure, threats or interferences, direct or indirect, from any quarter or for any reason."[9]

Where a defendant has selected trial by jury, the ultimate disposition of the case rests with the jurors and not with court officials. But the overall conduct of the trial is the responsibility of the presiding judge and jurors look to the judge for guidance and instruction on the complex legal issues before them. Any hint of bias from the bench may thus have a profound effect on the jury's deliberations.

The trial of Mumia Abu-Jamal was presided over by Judge Albert F. Sabo. His history of involvement with the police and law enforcement community has raised concerns that he was not the most suitable choice of official to oversee the trial of a defendant accused of killing a police officer. Albert Sabo was an Undersheriff of Philadelphia County for 16 years before becoming a judge in 1974. His official biography lists him as a former member of the National Sheriffs Association, "retired Fraternal Order of Police" (FOP) and as associated with the Police Chiefs' Association of South East Pennsylvania.[10] As a judge he was no stranger to the death penalty.

Over a period of 14 years, he presided over trials in which 31 defendants were sentenced to death, more than any other US judge as far as Amnesty International is aware. Of the 31 condemned defendants, 29 came from ethnic minorities.[11]

The judicial conduct of Judge Sabo has been a cause for concern to many members of the Philadelphia legal community for a number of years. A 1983 Philadelphia Bar survey found that over one third of the responding attorneys considered Judge Sabo unqualified to be on the bench. When asked about the survey, Judge Sabo appeared to reveal his bias against the defence by stating that if he were a defence attorney "I wouldn't vote for me either."

In 1992 the *Philadelphia Inquirer* reviewed 35 homicide trials presided over by Judge Sabo.[12] The investigation concluded that: "through his comments, his rulings and his instructions to the jury" Judge Sabo "favored prosecutors." According to the report, in one case, Judge Sabo even urged the prosecution to introduce evidence because "it would be helpful to [get] a conviction." A review of the court records by the *Inquirer* showed "that most of the homicide judges in Philadelphia hear more murder cases than Judge Sabo with fewer death sentences." In the same article, the *Inquirer* also concluded: "The assignment of a judge, like the naming of a lawyer, can be a life-or-death matter for a murder suspect. Some, like Judge Albert F. Sabo, are viewed as prosecution-minded. Others are seen as more favorable to defense. One report likened the system to a 'crap shoot'."

Throughout Abu-Jamal's trial—a trial to determine whether the defendant would live or die—Judge Sabo appeared to be more concerned with expediency than fairness. For example, during the proceedings of 17 June, he stated "I don't want to be held up on lousy technicalities...what do I care?" and "As far as I'm concerned, it can wait until lunchtime. Whatever you want to do, but let's do something. I have a jury waiting out there."

In 1995, defence lawyers requested that Judge Sabo recuse (i.e. remove) himself from presiding over an evidentiary hearing on whether Mumia Abu-Jamal's original trial was fair, on the grounds of "his inability to endow this proceeding with... the appearance of fairness and impartiality." Judge Sabo refused. During the hearing, he was openly hostile to the defence, causing one commentator to write: "[t]hroughout the internationally scrutinized post-conviction hearing, which ran from July 26 to August 15, and the closing arguments on September 11, Judge Sabo flaunted his bias, oozing partiality toward the prosecution and crudely seeking to bully Weinglass [a defence lawyer], whose courtroom conduct was as correct as Sabo's was crass."[13] On 16 July 1996, the *Philadelphia Inquirer* described Judge Sabo's adjudication of the hearings: "The behavior of the judge was disturbing first time around—and in hearings last week he did not give the impression to those in the courtroom of fair-mindedness. Instead, he gave the impression, damaging in the extreme, of undue haste and hostility toward the defense's case."

THE DEFENCE: MUMIA ABU-JAMAL'S LEGAL REPRESENTATION AT TRIAL

"They [defence lawyers] *must aid their clients in every appropriate way, taking such actions as is neces-*

sary to protect their clients' rights and interests, and assist their clients before the courts."[14]

US death penalty procedures are a uniquely complex area of criminal law, in which even attorneys experienced in non-capital trials may fail to adequately represent their clients. Amnesty International has documented numerous cases of death row prisoners who were represented at trial by woefully inadequate defence attorneys.[15] Its concern over such cases is shared by other international human rights groups and inter-governmental bodies. In 1996, for example, the International Commission of Jurists (ICJ), an international non-governmental organization which takes no position on the death penalty *per se*, published a report that was highly critical of the legal representation afforded defendants in capital cases, concluding: "the administration of the death penalty in the United States will remain arbitrary, and racially discriminatory, and prospects of a fair hearing for capital offenders cannot (and will not) be assured" without substantial remedial steps.[16] The UN Human Rights Committee (HRC—the expert body empowered to monitor countries' compliance with the International Covent on Civil and Political Rights—the ICCPR) has also made note of the concern over the "the lack of effective measures [in the USA] to ensure that indigent [poor] defendants in serious criminal proceedings, particularly in state courts, are represented by competent counsel."[17]

At the time of Mumia Abu-Jamal's trial, Pennsylvania had *no* minimum standards for those appointed to represent defendants on trial for their life. Attorneys in

capital cases were not required to pass any special examinations or to have reached any level of experience in
defending those facing trial on serious charges.[18]

Mumia Abu-Jamal was initially represented by a
court-appointed attorney, Anthony Jackson. At a pretrial
hearing on 13 May 1982, Abu-Jamal requested the court's
permission to represent himself at trial because he was
dissatisfied with Jackson's performance.[19] Judge Ribner,
the judge overseeing the pre-trial hearings, granted his
request but, over Abu-Jamal's vigorous objection,
appointed Jackson as backup counsel. Jackson also
protested at being appointed as backup counsel, stating
that he did not know what it entailed, but was told by
the judge; "You can fight that out with Mr. Jamal." Jackson was given no clarification by the court as to his role
in the trial as backup counsel.

Since Mumia Abu-Jamal was obviously unable to
conduct investigations due to his continued detention,
his access to a fully prepared lawyer—even as "backup
counsel"—was vital to ensure a fair hearing. In a sworn
affidavit dated 17 April 1995, Jackson admitted to being
"unprepared" for trial and that he "abandoned all efforts
at trial preparation" three weeks before the start of the
trial after Mumia Abu-Jamal had obtained the right to
represent himself.

During jury selection on the third day of the trial, at
the suggestion of the prosecution, Judge Sabo withdrew
permission for Mumia Abu-Jamal to act as his own attorney—supposedly only for the duration of jury selection.
Judge Sabo based this decision on Abu-Jamal's alleged
slowness in questioning potential jurors and on the

grounds that his status as an accused murderer instilled fear and anxiety in the jurors. However, Judge Sabo did concede that .".it is true I have not rebuked Mr. Jamal at any time [during jury selection]."

Jackson objected to the ruling, pointing out to Judge Sabo that "The last case I had before you, it took us nine days to select a jury and it certainly didn't have as much publicity as this case." Jackson noted that jury selection in another homicide case had taken five weeks to complete. He went on to state that "in all homicide cases, particularly in capital cases... jurors express some apprehension, some unsettlement, some fear with regard to the whole process." These objections were to no avail, Judge Sabo continued to deny Abu-Jamal the right to represent himself.

The *Philadelphia Inquirer* described Abu-Jamal's conduct prior to his removal as lead counsel as "intent and business like" and "subdued." In the first two days of the trial, Abu-Jamal had questioned 23 prospective jurors, successfully challenging two for "cause" (bias), defeating a prosecution challenge for cause, and exercising two peremptory strikes (the right to remove a prospective juror without giving reasons).

Amnesty International's own examination of the trial transcript found no justifiable reason for the revoking of Mumia Abu-Jamal's right to question potential jurors. At no point during his questioning was he rude or aggressive and his examinations are very similar, in terms of length, to those of the prosecution. His questions were pertinent to the selection of a fair jury. The removal of Abu-Jamal's right to represent himself at this point in the trial is not supported in any way by the record of the trial. Judge Sabo's comment that "You have indicated to this court that you do not have the expertise necessary to conduct *voir dire*" (jury selection) is likewise not supported by the record.

After the jury had been selected and the trial proper began, Mumia Abu-Jamal resumed representing himself. However, the already tense relations between him and Judge Sabo deteriorated rapidly. It is clear from the exchanges between the two men that Abu-Jamal had come to the conclusion that he would be denied a fair trial by the court. His repeated requests to be legally represented by John Africa were denied by Judge Sabo, on the grounds that Africa was not a licensed attorney.[20] Mumia Abu-Jamal also requested that John Africa be allowed to sit at the defence table, in order to provide legal and tactical advice throughout the trial. This request was permissible under Pennsylvania law but was denied by Judge Sabo. When pressed by Abu-Jamal, who gave examples of other judges who had allowed non-lawyers to sit at the table of defendants, Judge Sabo stated that unless there was a legal precedent, he did not care what other judges did, and continued to refuse the request. Typical of the exchanges between Judge Sabo and Mumia Abu-Jamal is the following:

Judge Sabo: *Mr. Jamal, it is quite evident to this court that you are intentionally disrupting the orderly procedure of this court. I have warned you time and again that if you continue with that attitude that I would have to remove you as counsel in this case.*

Mumia Abu-Jamal: *Judge, your warnings to me are absolutely meaningless. I'm here fighting for my life. Do you understand that? I'm not fighting to please the Court, or to please the DA, I'm fighting for my life. I need counsel of choice, someone I have faith in, someone I have respect for; not someone paid by the same pocket that pays the DA, not a court-appointed lawyer, not a member of the ABA, not an officer of the court but someone I can trust and I have faith in. Your warnings are absolutely moot, they're meaningless to me.*

Shortly after this exchange, Judge Sabo prohibited Mumia Abu-Jamal from representing himself in court and Jackson was reappointed lead counsel. Jackson protested, but his request to be removed was rejected by Judge Sabo, who threatened the lawyer with disciplinary action, including imprisonment for contempt of court, unless he continued.[21] This left the defendant represented by a lawyer who was both reluctant to participate and ill-prepared for trial, effectively stripping Mumia Abu-Jamal of any meaningful legal representation. The following day, after a number of other angry exchanges between judge and defendant, Judge Sabo had Abu-Jamal physically removed from the courtroom.

For the remainder of the trial, Mumia Abu-Jamal was continuously readmitted to and removed from the trial. His behaviour in the courtroom became highly belligerent and disruptive to the proceedings, leaving Judge Sabo with little choice but to remove him if the trial were to continue. However, even if his behaviour justi-

fied the court in excluding Abu-Jamal from many of the
critical parts of the trial, it would not release the presiding authorities from the duty to conduct a fair and
impartial trial and from ensuring that his exclusion
infringed as little as possible on Abu-Jamal's right to participate in his own defence. In effect, Mumia Abu-Jamal
was tried *in absentia* during a large portion of the trial.

THE RIGHT TO THE RESOURCES NECESSARY FOR AN ADEQUATE DEFENCE

*During the proceedings, every person is entitled...to
obtain the appearance, as witnesses, of experts or other
persons who may throw light on the facts.*[22]

Mumia Abu-Jamal's lack of meaningful legal representation was compounded by the refusal of Judge Ribner, the pre-trial judge, to grant the defence adequate
funds to employ an investigator, pathologist or ballistics
expert. The court also refused defence attorney Jackson
requests for a second attorney to aid the defence.[23] In
response to the initial request for funds, the Court allocated $150 for each expert. On three occasions, the
defence attempted to have this amount increased as it
was proving impossible to obtain expert evaluation of the
evidence for this fee. On each occasion this entirely reasonable request was denied. Jackson explained to Judge
Ribner that he was experiencing difficulties in recruit-
ing the experts without the guarantee of funding. The
judge replied that if Jackson submitted an itemised bill
for the work the judge would approve payment, assum-
ing he found the charges reasonable. Jackson pointed out

that he had told the experts this but that they were still not willing to work without an advance payment—to which the judge replied: "Tell them, 'The Calendar judge said 'trust me'."[24]

This sum allocated by the courts to cover Jackson's fees and expenses for his work on the case for over six months, payment for an investigator to locate and interview witnesses, and fees for experts to evaluate the evidence and testify in court concerning their findings, was clearly insufficient. The defence presented **no** expert testimony on ballistics or pathology.[25] The police and prosecution interviewed more than 100 witnesses during their investigation of the crime. The evaluation of these statements alone would have taken more time than Jackson could afford to devote to them.

THE JURY: A FAIR AND IMPARTIAL PANEL OF ABU-JAMAL'S PEERS?

An essential element of a fair trial is the selection of an impartial jury of the defendant's peers, one which will base its verdict solely on the evidence presented to it. Where a case generates a high degree of controversy and publicity, trial courts routinely grant a change of venue, to ensure that the jury has not been exposed to pretrial publicity that could bias its deliberations. Of approximately 80 people in the jury pool at Mumia Abu-Jamal's trial, all but seven prospective jurors admitted that they were familiar with media coverage of the case.

The jury eventually selected (including the four alternate jurors[26]) consisted of two blacks and 14 whites. The population of Philadelphia at the time of the trial was

40 per cent African American; a jury racially representative of the community could thus have been expected
to include at least five black members.

The prosecution used 11 out of its 15 peremptory
strikes to remove African Americans from the jury. In
1986, the US Supreme Court ruled in the case of *Batson
v. Kentucky* that the removal of potential jurors must
be "race neutral."[27]

The jurors selected for the trial of Mumia Abu-Jamal
appear to have received different treatment from the court
according to their race. Jennie Dawley, black, was the
only juror selected while Abu-Jamal was conducting his
own defence. Dawley requested, before the trial started,
that she be allowed to take her sick cat to the veterinarian
during the evening, thereby not disrupting the court proceedings.[28] Judge Sabo denied this request without
informing the defence. Juror Dawley was dismissed from
the jury when she failed to abide by the Court's instruction. In contrast, a white juror requested permission to
take a civil service exam during court time. Judge Sabo
granted this request, temporarily halted the trial and
instructed a court official to accompany the juror and
ensure that he saw no media coverage of the trial.

The removal of jurors by the prosecution on the
grounds of their race remains a common practice. Prosecutors simply give a vaguely plausible non-racial reason for dismissing the juror.

One year after the *Batson* ruling, the Assistant District Attorney for Philadelphia made a training videotape
for the city's prosecutors. On the video, he describes how

to select a jury more likely to convict, including the removal of potential black jurors: "Let's face it, the blacks from the low-income areas are less likely to convict. There's a resentment to law enforcement... You don't want those guys on your jury... If you get a white teacher in a black school who's sick of these guys, that may be the one to accept."

The video also instructed the trainee prosecutors on how to hide the racial motivation for the rejection of prospective jurors in order to avoid successful claims of racial discrimination from defence lawyers. The tape did not become public until 1997.

A recent study of Philadelphia found that the likelihood of receiving a death sentence is nearly four times higher if the defendant is black. See *Killing with Prejudice* for more details.

Jennie Dawley was replaced by a white alternate juror, Robert Courchain. On at least five occasions during jury selection, Courchain stated that, although he would try, he might be unable to set aside his bias in the case. For example, he stated: "unconsciously I don't think I could be fair to both sides." The defence sought the removal of Courchain "for cause" (i.e. that he was incapable of deliberating impartially), but Judge Sabo denied the request. As Jackson had previously used the one peremptory strike available to him at this point he was unable to prevent Courchain from becoming an alternate juror.

Jackson also allowed two jurors onto the jury whose life experiences could possibly prejudice them against

Abu-Jamal. Juror number 11 was the close friend of a police officer who had been shot while on duty. While being questioned, he openly admitted that this experience could mean he was unable to be a fair juror because of his feelings concerning his friend. Juror number 15 (an alternate) was the wife of a serving police officer. Jackson allowed both onto the jury without objection.

THE CASE FOR THE PROSECUTION: TOO MANY UNRESOLVED QUESTIONS

At trial, the prosecution's case against Abu-Jamal consisted of three elements:

➤the 'confession' allegedly made by Abu-Jamal at the hospital;
➤three eyewitnesses who testified that they saw Abu-Jamal commit the offence;
➤the presence of Abu-Jamal's gun at the murder scene, which the prosecution alleged was the murder weapon.

MUMIA ABU-JAMAL'S "CONFESSION"

"One can have eyewitness testimonial evidence, circumstantial evidence, scientific evidence, and even video evidence; but a confession explicitly admitting guilt...is the most powerful piece of evidence that can ever be introduced against him and will surely serve as the key that locks the jail-house door and provides the juice to power the electric chair; and in these more civilized times, the juice for the needle." Judge Overstreet, Texas Court of Criminal Appeals.[29]

During the trial, the jury heard testimony from hospital security guard Priscilla Durham and police officer Gary Bell.[30] According to both witnesses, when about to receive treatment for his bullet wound at the hospital, Mumia Abu-Jamal stated: "I shot the motherfucker, and I hope the motherfucker dies."

During an appeal court hearing in 1995, a third witness, police officer Gary Wakshul, also claimed to have heard the statement. However, Officer Wakshul, who was in the police vehicle that took Mumia Abu-Jamal to the hospital, had written in his report that "we stayed with the male at Jefferson [hospital] until we were relieved. During this time, the negro male made no comments."

None of the many other police officers in and around the hospital treatment room at that time claimed to have heard the statement, which Abu-Jamal allegedly shouted. Doctors who treated Abu-Jamal at the hospital stated in their testimony that they were with him from the moment he arrived, that he was "weak...on the verge of fainting," and that they did not hear him make any statement that could be interpreted as a confession.

None of the three witnesses to the alleged confession reported what they had claimed to have heard until February 1982, more than two months after the shooting. They reported the alleged incriminating statements during interviews with the police Internal Affairs Unit. The interviews took place after Abu-Jamal's made allegations of being abused by the police when he was arrested.[31]

Officer Wakshul claimed that his delay in reporting the confession was due to "emotional trauma" caused by the murder of Officer Faulkner. The two other witnesses stated that they did not believe the outburst was significant enough to report to the police.

However, during her trial testimony, Priscilla Durham claimed that she had reported the statement to her hospital supervisor the day after the events and that they had prepared a *handwritten* note of her allegation. Upon hearing this testimony, the prosecution sent an officer to the hospital in an attempt to recover the supervisor's record of Durham's statement. The officer returned from the hospital with an unsigned *typewritten* statement, which Priscilla Durham denied having seen before. Despite finding that this was not the original document, that the witness had not seen it before that day, and that its authenticity was not verified, Judge Sabo allowed it into evidence. He conjectured that "They took the handwritten statement and typed this"—events that were not in evidence and that he was thus not in a position to deduce.

Gary Wakshul, the officer who noted in his report that "during this time, the male negro made no statements," did not testify at the trial. When the defence lawyer attempted to call him as a witness, it transpired that he was on holiday, despite a notation on a police investigation report that Wakshul was not permitted to be on leave at the time of the trial. The defence requested that Officer Wakshul's whereabouts be established or that the trial be temporarily halted to enable them to locate him. That request was denied by Judge Sabo, who commented to Mumia Abu-Jamal that "your attorney and you goofed."

The jury was never informed of the existence of Officer Wakshul's written report of his custody of Mumia Abu-Jamal which clearly contradicts the claim that the suspect "confessed" to killing Officer Faulkner. Therefore, the jury was left with little reason to doubt the testimony of the two witnesses who claimed to have heard the confession.

The likelihood of two police officers and a security guard forgetting or neglecting to report the confession of a suspect in the killing of another police officer for more than two months strains credulity. Priscilla Durham's claim that she believed Mumia Abu-Jamal's "confession" was important enough to report to her supervisor (who in turn thought it important enough to have typed out from the original handwritten version) but not important enough to notify the police is scarcely credible.

In a conversation with an Amnesty International researcher, one of Mumia Abu-Jamal's current legal team stated that a number of the jurors have told defence investigators that they had taken into consideration Abu-Jamal's "confession," not just in deciding his guilt but also in sentencing him to death, since the statement portrayed him as aggressive and callous. However, the jurors refused to make any public statements to this effect. The concern remains that a possibly fabricated "confession" may have been a major contributing factor in the jury sentencing Mumia Abu-Jamal to death.

WITNESSES TO THE CRIME: CONFLICTING AND CONFUSING

During the trial, three witnesses testified that Abu-Jamal had run up to Officer Faulkner, shot him in the back and then stood over him and fired another bullet into his head, killing him instantly (although only one witness, White, claimed to have seen the events as described above in their entirety). None of the witnesses testified that Faulkner fired at Abu-Jamal as he fell to the ground—even when specifically asked—as the prosecution maintained. The prosecution also maintained that only Abu-Jamal, his brother William Cook and Officer Faulkner were present in the immediate vicinity of the crime scene.

In the years since the trial, defence lawyers have thrown into doubt the reliability of much of this trial testimony.

The complicated nature of the numerous accusations, counter accusations and withdrawing of statements and testimony make it impossible, based on the existing record, to reach definitive conclusions regarding the reliability of any witness. The prosecutors and police contend that the testimony presented at the trial was truthful and uncoerced, and that other witnesses to the crime were not called to testify as they had nothing relevant to add.

However, Abu-Jamal's attorneys contend that a number of witnesses changed their original statements regarding what they saw on the night of the crime after being coerced, threatened or offered inducements by the police. Based on a comparison of their statements given to the police immediately after the shooting, their testimony during pretrial hearings and their testimony at the trial, the key witnesses did substantively alter their descriptions of what they saw, in ways that supported the prosecution's version of events.

CYNTHIA WHITE AND VERONICA JONES

Cynthia White was a prostitute working in the area on the night in question. At the trial she testified that she had seen Mumia Abu-Jamal run up to Officer Faulkner, shoot him in the back, and then stand over him firing at his head.

Prior to the trial, White had given four written statements and one tape-recorded statement to the police. In one interview she estimated the height of the person who shot Faulkner to be shorter than five feet eight inches. Abu-Jamal is six feet one inch tall. In her first court appearance at a pretrial hearing, she testified that Abu-Jamal held the gun in his left hand. Three days later she testified that she was unsure which hand he held the gun in. At trial she denied knowing which hand the gun was in. During her trial testimony, she claimed that the diagram she originally drew of the incident was incorrect and that her placement of the actors prior to Abu-Jamal's appearance was inaccurate.

There is evidence to show that Cynthia White received preferential treatment from the prosecution and police. At the time of the trial, she was serving an 18-month prison sentence for prostitution in Massachusetts. She had 38 previous arrests for prostitution in Philadelphia; three of those charges were still pending at the time of trial. She was arrested twice within days of the shooting incident (12 and 17 December). According to Abu-Jamal's current defence attorneys, there are no records of White ever being prosecuted for those arrests.

In 1987, a detective involved in the prosecution of Abu-Jamal testified in support of bail for White at a court hearing concerning charges of robbery, aggravated assault and possession of illegal weapons. Despite the judge pointing out that White had failed to appear in court on 17 different occasions and that she had "page after page" of arrests and convictions, the prosecution consented to the request that she be allowed to sign her own bail and the judge released her. According to information received by Amnesty International, White failed to appear in court on the charges and the authorities have since been unable to locate her. At an appeal hearings in 1997, the prosecution claimed Cynthia White was deceased and produced a 1992 death certificate in the name of Cynthia Williams, claiming that the fingerprints of the dead woman and White matched. However, an examination of the fingerprint records of White and Williams showed no match and the evidence that White is now dead is far from conclusive.

A second prostitute, Veronica Jones, witnessed the killing and testified for the defence. She claimed she had been offered inducements by the police to testify that she saw Abu-Jamal kill Faulkner, stating that "they [the police] were trying to get me to say something the other girl [White] said. I couldn't do that." Jones went on to testify that "they [the police] told us we could work the area [as prostitutes] if we tell them [that Abu-Jamal was the shooter]."

However, Judge Sabo had the jury removed for this testimony and then ruled that Jones' statements were inadmissible evidence. The jury were thus left unaware of the allegations that police officers were offering inducements in return for testimony against Abu-Jamal. In her testimony before the jury, Jones retracted her original statement to police that she saw two unidentified men leave the scene of the crime. Remarkably, Jackson had never interviewed his own witness (a standard practice) but Jones was interviewed by the prosecution prior to the trial.

In 1996, Veronica Jones testified at an appeal hearing that she changed her version of events after being visited by two police officers in prison, where she was being held on charges of robbery and assault. While cross-examining Jones, the prosecution announced to the court that there was an outstanding arrest warrant for Jones on charges of passing bad cheques and indicated that she would be arrested at the conclusion of her testimony.

In a sworn affidavit, Jones described her meeting with the plain clothes police officers:

> "They told me that if I would testify against Jamal and identify Jamal as the shooter I wouldn't have to worry about my pending felony charges...The detectives threatened me by reminding me that I faced a long prison sentence

—fifteen years...I knew that if I did anything to help the Jamal defense I would face years in prison."

After Abu-Jamal's trial, Veronica Jones received a sentence of two years' probation on the charges she was facing.

In January 1997, another former prostitute who worked in the area of the crime scene in 1981, came forward. In a sworn affidavit, Pamela Jenkins stated that she knew Cynthia White, who had told her she was afraid of the police and that the police were trying to get her to say something about the shooting of Faulkner and had threatened her life. Jenkins was the lover and informant of Philadelphia police officer Tom Ryan. In her statement, Jenkins claimed that Ryan "wanted me to perjure myself and say that I had seen Jamal shoot the police officer." In 1996, Tom Ryan and five other officers from the same district went to prison after being convicted of charges of planting evidence, stealing money from suspects and making false reports. Their convictions resulted in the release of numerous prisoners implicated by the officers. Jenkins was a principal prosecution witness at the trials of the officers.

ROBERT CHOBERT

Robert Chobert had just let a passenger out of his cab and was parked when he viewed the incident. It is undisputed that he was closest to the scene of the prosecution eyewitnesses, parked in his cab a car's length behind Faulkner's police car and approximately 50 feet from the shooting. According to his testimony and statements, he was writing in his logbook when he heard the first shot and looked up. He had to look over or past Faulkner's car, with its flashing red dome light, to see the incident and saw the shooter only in profile. Chobert testified at trial that when he looked up, he saw Faulkner fall and then saw Abu-Jamal "standing over him and firing some more shots into him. "Under cross-examination by Jackson, he stated: "I know who shot the cop, and I ain't going to forget it."

But Chobert's first recorded statement to police—about which the jury was not told—was that the shooter "apparently ran away," according to a report written on 10 December 1981 by Inspector Giordano. Giordano encountered Chobert upon reaching the scene about five minutes after the shooting. Giordano wrote: "[A] white male from the crowd stated that he saw the shooting and that a black MOVE member had done it and appearently [sic] ran away. When asked what he ment [sic] bby [sic] a MOVE member, the white male stated, 'His hair, his hair,' appearantly [sic] referring to dreadlocks."

There are also discrepancies between Chobert's description of the shooter's clothes and weight and that of Abu-Jamal.

During the trial, Jackson attempted to introduce into evidence Chobert's previous convictions for driving while intoxicated (twice) and the arson of a school, for which he was on probation. Jackson sought to introduce the convictions to challenge Chobert's credibility, but Judge Sabo refused to allow the defence the opportunity to make the jury aware of Chobert's convictions.

The jury were also left unaware that Chobert had been driving his cab with a suspended drivers' license on the night of the killing; that it was still suspended at the time of the trial and that the police had never sought to charge him for this offence. According to Chobert's testimony at the 1995 hearing, he had asked the prosecutor during the trial "if he could help me find out how I could get my license back," which was "important" to him because "that's how I earned my living." According to Chobert, the prosecutor told him that he would "look into it."

During this final summation to the jury, the prosecutor emphasized Chobert's testimony, telling the jury they could "trust" Chobert because "he knows what he saw." The prosecutor suggested that Chobert's testimony was given without anyone having influenced him, telling the jury: "do you think that anybody could get him to say anything that wasn't the truth? I would not criticize that man one bit...What motivation would Robert Chobert have to make up a story...." However, subsequent revelations suggest that Chobert had substantial reasons to ingratiate himself with the authorities by corroborating their version of events.

MARK SCANLAN

In one of his original statements to the police, Scanlan stated several times that he did not know whether Abu-Jamal or his brother shot Faulkner: "I don't know who had the gun. I don't know who fired it." He also misidentified Abu-Jamal as the driver of the vehicle stopped by Officer Faulkner and was approximately 120 feet from the scene. A diagram that Scanlan drew for police indicated that Abu-Jamal and Faulkner were facing each other when the first shot was fired, contrary to the prosecution's theory that the police officer was initially shot in the back. At trial, Scanlan admitted that he had been drinking on the night in question and that "There was confusion when all three of them were in front of the car."

THE MISSING WITNESSES

Abu-Jamal's attorneys also allege that a number of eye witnesses were not investigated by the defence because of a lack of resources and that the witnesses' whereabouts were withheld from them by the prosecution. According to subsequent investigations by the current defence team, numerous witnesses have been located who claim to have seen other unidentified men fleeing the scene of the killing. Since this report is primarily concerned with the fairness of Abu-Jamal's original trial, Amnesty International has not analysed the statements of these potential witnesses. The defence filed an appellate brief in Federal court in October 1999 which summarizes these claims.[32]

William Cook, Abu-Jamal's brother and an obvious eyewitness to the killing, did not testify for either side at trial. He was convicted in separate proceedings of assaulting Faulkner. Cook made a statement to the police on the night of the shooting, and another to Abu-Jamal's legal team in 1995. However, neither of these statements have been seen by Amnesty International. Abu-Jamal's supporters have alleged that in 1982, Cook was being intimidated by the police and feared being charged in connection with the killing and was therefore too frightened to testify. Cook was scheduled to testify during the 1995 hearing but failed to appear. Again it was alleged that this was due to fear of the police and of being arrested on unrelated charges in court. In his written denial of the 1995 appeal, Judge Sabo made negative assumptions regarding Cook's unwillingness to testify. Since 1995, the defence team have been unable to locate Cook despite numerous attempts.

THE BALLISTICS EVIDENCE

Although all five bullets in Abu-Jamal's gun were spent, the police failed to conduct tests to ascertain whether the weapon had been fired in the immediate past. The test is relatively simple: smell the gun for the odour of gun powder, which should be detectable for approximately five hours after the gun was fired. Compounding this error, the police also failed to conduct chemical tests on Abu-Jamal's hands to find out if he had fired a gun recently.

The police appeared to be aware of the value of basic forensic testing. According to the testimony of Arnold Howard during the 1995 hearings, after he was arrested on suspicion of involvement in the Faulkner shooting, the police tested his hands to ascertain if he had fired a gun in the recent past. Howard was arrested because his driver's license application form was in Faulkner's possession.

As noted on page 12, the court refused to grant the defence funding sufficient to obtain expert witnesses. As a consequence, the jury was presented with no expert testimony to counter the prosecution's assertion that Abu-Jamal had fired at Officer Faulkner and that the policeman was killed with Abu-Jamal's weapon.

The prosecution maintained that Officer Faulkner turned and fired at Abu-Jamal as he fell to the ground after being shot. Therefore, the entry of the bullet into Abu-Jamal should have been on a level or upward trajectory. However, according to the medical records, the overall pathway of the bullet was downwards. During trial, the doctor who removed the bullet from Abu-Jamal (who admitted his lack of forensic expertise) was asked why the bullet would be "unnecessarily lowered in its trajectory" and speculated that "ricochet" and "tumble" were the explanation.

In 1992, an expert forensic pathologist employed by Abu-Jamal's defence team examined the medical records and concluded:

> "...For these reasons, there appears to be no reasons to postulate a ricochet to explain a downward course through the body. Rather, it is likely that the bullet had a downward course through the body because of the relative positions of Mr. Jamal and the shooter. Consistent relative positions include a standing shooter firing down on a prone Mr. Jamal, or a standing shooter firing horizontally at Mr. Jamal while Mr. Jamal was bent over at the waist."

Neither of these postures is consistent with the prosecution's theory. The forensic pathologist also concluded that "since I disagree with both the Medical Examiner's findings with respect to the cause of death and Dr. Coletta's postulation of a possible 'ricochet'...Mr. Jamal's defense required, and would have been well served by, the testimony of a qualified forensic pathologist."

There were also inconsistencies in the original findings concerning the bullet removed from Faulkner's body. The Medical Examiner first wrote in his notes that the bullet was ."44 cal." (Abu-Jamal's gun was a .38 calibre weapon and could not possibly have fired such a bullet). This discrepancy, which was never made known to the jury, was later explained by the Medical Examiner as "part of the paper work but not an official finding." At trial, the Medical Examiner testified that the bullet was consistent with the those fired by Abu-Jamal's gun but that test were inconclusive as to whether it actually came from his firearm. The court accepted the medical examiner as a ballistics expert. However, during the 1995 hearing, Judge Sabo contended that the medical examiner was "not a ballistics expert"" and that his original findings that the bullet was a .44 calibre were a "mere lay guess."

In a case where the prosecution's theory of the crime rests on a specific sequence of events involving an exchange of gunfire, the gathering of ballistics evidence is crucial—as is the ability of the defence to present its own expert testimony on the significance of that evidence. The failure of the police to test Abu-Jamal's gun, hands and clothing for evidence of recent firing is deeply troubling. Without the ability to hear and assess that missing evidence, the jury was required to reach a verdict based largely on the contradictory and variable testimony of a limited list of eye witnesses.

THE SENTENCE: CONDEMNED TO DEATH BY FREE SPEECH?

All persons are equal before the law...In this respect, the law shall prohibit any discrimination and guarantee all persons equal and effective protection against discrimination on any grounds such as...political or other opinions...[33]

Following a guilty verdict in a death penalty case, the majority of trial courts in the USA are required to convene a separate penalty phase hearing, during which the prosecution and defence present evidence and testimony arguing for and against a sentence of death. If the jury finds that the aggravating factors supporting execution outweigh the mitigating factors supporting leniency, they are required to impose a death sentence. Under Pennsylvania law, if even one juror disagrees with that finding a death sentence may not be imposed.

Like so much of Mumia Abu-Jamal's trial, the penalty phase was hurried and brief, lasting less than two hours. The jury then took less than three and a half hours to deliberate over Abu-Jamal's sentence.[34]

Although Abu-Jamal took the witness stand during the penalty phase, he limited his statements to objecting to various aspects of the trial that he believed were unfair and prejudicial to him, and to asserting his innocence. While his decision to testify as he did may thus have diminished his prospects for a life sentence, Jackson's defence of Abu-Jamal at this crucial phase of the trial was virtually nonexistent. He called no character witnesses, despite the availability of a State Representative for Philadelphia who would have testified concerning Abu-Jamal's "positive influence on the community" and "his advocacy respecting the need for the different ethnic and racial communities to work in harmony."[35] At no point did Jackson discuss a strategy for developing mitigating factors before the jury with Abu-Jamal's mother and sister, both of whom were prepared to testify on his behalf.

During the penalty phase, the prosecution used Mumia Abu-Jamal's purported political beliefs and statements he made as a teenager against him. These statements were made 12 years before the trial and had no bearing on the case. The prosecution quoted from remarks attributed to Abu-Jamal in a newspaper article when he was a 16-year-old member of the Black Panther Party, which included the quotation from Mao Tse Tung that "political power grows out of the barrel of a gun." When questioning Abu-Jamal about his statements, the prosecutor suggested the remark "might ring a bell as to whether or not you are an executioner or endorse such actions."

During his summation of the case to the jury, the prosecutor cited Mumia Abu-Jamal's alleged political statements as a youth to argue for a death sentence, surmising that the defendant had held a long-standing desire to kill a police officer. The prosecutor clearly implied that Mumia Abu-Jamal's statements indicated his potential to kill a police officer:

"Anybody can grasp or hold any kind of philosophy you want. That's fine. That's what this country happens to be all made of. But, one thing that cannot be tolerated is constant abuse of authority and daily law breaking. That simply is not permitted."

THE SECRET MONITORING OF MUMIA ABU-JAMAL

In 1995, defence lawyers obtained approximately 700 pages of files on Mumia Abu-Jamal maintained by the Federal Bureau of Investigation (FBI), via the Freedom of Information Act. These documents represented only a portion of the total files and were heavily censored.

The FBI began monitoring Abu-Jamal in 1969 when he was 15 years old, because of his activities at High School and later with the Black Panther Party (BPP). According to a sworn affidavit by the attorney who examined the files, Abu-Jamal was under surveillance as part of the FBI's Counterintelligence Program, COIN-TELPRO (see footnote 7), which operated with the cooperation and assistance of the Philadelphia police. According to the affidavit: "Mr. Jamal was subjected to surveillance, harassment, disruption, politically motivated arrests and attempted frame-ups by the FBI, who worked in conjunction with the Philadelphia Police Department." Although the FBI classified Abu-Jamal as "armed and dangerous," he was not convicted of any crime during this period. The documents reveal that the FBI was continuing to monitor Abu-Jamal as late as 1990, recording the details of one of his visitors while he was incarcerated. Huntingdon Prison.

Given that Mumia Abu-Jamal had no prior convictions for any offence, or any history of involvement in politically motivated violence, this reasoning was highly prejudicial and improper.

The US Supreme Court has determined that the prosecution's use of a defendant's political beliefs during the sentencing phase of a death penalty trial violates the US Constitution's First Amendment: the right to freedom of speech. In *Dawson v Delaware* (1992), the Court ruled that the prosecution's introduction of Dawson's membership of a "white racist prison gang" (the Aryan Brotherhood) during the penalty phase was unconstitutional. "Whatever label is given to the evidence presented... Dawson's First Amendment rights were violated by the admission of the Aryan Brotherhood evidence...because the evidence proved nothing more than Dawson's abstract beliefs," the Supreme Court ruled.

Amnesty International believes that *any* risk that the jury may have been improperly influenced in favour of the death penalty is unacceptable and should constitute grounds for reversing Abu-Jamal's death sentence.

THE APPEAL TO THE PENNSYLVANIA SUPREME COURT

Mumia Abu-Jamal first appealed his conviction and sentence to the Pennsylvania Supreme Court in 1989, citing a number of errors and irregularities in the trial proceedings. The appeal was denied on all grounds.

The Court found no error in the prosecutor's references in his summation to Mumia Abu-Jamal's past

political affiliations and statements. The Court denied
the appeal, ruling that "Punishing a person for express-
ing his views or for associating with certain people is
substantially different from allowing...evidence of [the
defendant's] character [to be considered] where that character is a relevant inquiry." The Delaware Supreme
Court cited, and adopted verbatim, the Pennsylvania
Supreme Court's ruling in the Abu-Jamal case to deny
the appeal of Delaware death row prisoner, David Dawson. It would now appear that the US Supreme Court has
found fault with the Pennsylvania Supreme Court's
logic, through its ruling in *Dawson v. Delaware.*

The Pennsylvania Supreme Court also rejected
Mumia Abu-Jamal's claim that the prosecutor had acted
improperly when he had attempted to lessen the jury's
responsibility for imposing a death sentence by referring
to the lengthy appeals process, telling them:

> "Ladies and gentleman, you are not asked to
> kill anybody. You are asked to follow the law. The
> same law that I keep throwing at you, saying
> those words, law and order. I should point out to
> you it's the same law that has for six months pro-
> vided safeguards for this defendant. The same law
> that will provide him appeal after appeal after
> appeal...[because of] the same law...nobody has
> died in Pennsylvania since 1962."

In a previous case also presided over by Judge Sabo
(*Commonwealth v Baker*), and involving the same prosecutor, Joseph McGill, the prosecution also described the

lengthy appeals of death row inmates in his summation to the jury. In 1986 the Pennsylvania Supreme Court overturned Baker's death sentence, on the grounds that such language "minimiz[ed] the jury's sense of responsibility for a verdict of death."[36] The court then reversed this precedent in 1989 by upholding Abu-Jamal's death sentence, only to reestablish it in 1990, in the case of *Commonwealth v Beasley*, ordering the "precluding of all remarks about the appellate process in all future trials." This contradictory series of precedents leaves the disturbing impression that the Court invented a new standard of procedure to apply it to one case only: that of Mumia Abu-Jamal.

Abu-Jamal's appeal also argued that the withdrawal of the court's permission for the defendant to represent himself violated his constitutional rights. In response, the Pennsylvania Supreme Court stated: "The trial court noted at the time of *voir dire* [jury selection] that several of the potential jurors were obviously shaken by Appellant's questioning. Appellant also refused to adhere to proper procedure during this *voir dire...*" This conclusion is not supported by the trial transcript.

The Court further held that Abu-Jamal did not have a guaranteed right to self-representation, since indigent defendants do not have the right to a lawyer of their own choosing:

"While an accused is constitutionally guaranteed the right to the assistance of counsel that right gives to a defendant only the right to choose, at his or her own cost, any attorney desired. Where, as here, an accused is indigent, the right involves counsel, but not free counsel of choice." (Emphasis in original.)

The Pennsylvania Supreme Court also denied Abu-Jamal's claim that the trial court's failure to require Officer Wakshul to testify amounted to a violation of a defendant's right to call exculpatory witnesses (i.e. witnesses that would help to prove his innocence). The Court based its decision on four grounds: Wakshul's claim that he had not reported the confession because he was in an emotional state over the death of Faulkner had been found credible by Judge Sabo and the state Supreme court Justices had no reason to doubt that finding; Wakshul's account of the events was independent of Priscilla Durham's statement; Jackson's failure to call Wakshul at an earlier time, thereby ensuring his appearance in court, did not amount to "ineffective assistance of counsel" because it was Abu-Jamal's decision to call the witness at the last minute and that Wakshul's testimony would have damaged Abu-Jamal by confirming the other two witnesses account of the "confession."

By failing to compel Officer Wakshul to testify, the courts deprived the defence of the opportunity to cross-examine a key witness whose initial report of Abu-Jamal's behaviour at the hospital is blatantly contradicted by his subsequent statements. Without hearing his sworn testimony, the jury was unable to properly assess the credibility of a central element of the prosecution's case: Abu-Jamal's alleged "confession." As discussed above on page 17, the jury's response to the alleged confession may have played a pivotal role in their deliberations during both phases of the trial.

In October 1998, the Pennsylvania Supreme Court denied Abu-Jamal's last appeal in state court. The case is now entering the federal court system for the final stages of appellate review.

Concern has been raised over the strong links between members of the Pennsylvanian Supreme Court and the local law enforcement community, as well as the previous involvement of one member of the Court in the prosecution of Mumia Abu-Jamal. These unresolved concerns and the Court's own rulings on Abu-Jamal's appeals have left the unfortunate impression that the state Supreme Court may have been unable to impartially adjudicate this controversial case.

Prior to the Court ruling on Abu-Jamal's appeal in 1998, his attorneys requested that Justice Ron Castille not participate in the deliberations. Justice Castille is a former Philadelphia District Attorney who opposed Abu-Jamal's earlier appeals; as the District Attorney, his name appeared on the appeal briefs which expressly advocated the position that Abu-Jamal's trial was fair and that the evidence against him was compelling. He was openly endorsed by the Fraternal Order of Police (FOP) for election to the Supreme Court. When refusing to recuse himself, Justice Castille made the following statement:

> "I note that the very same FOP which endorsed me during earlier electoral processes also endorsed Mr. Chief Justice John P. Flaherty,

Mr. Justice Ralph Cappy, Mr. Justice Russell M. Nigro, and Madame Justice Sandra Schultz Newman. If the FOP's endorsement constituted a basis for recusal, practically the entire court would be required to decline participation in this appeal."

The refusal of a judge to recuse himself from proceedings in which he previously served as an advocate for one of the parties is a serious breach of judicial ethics. Amnesty International deeply regrets Judge Castille's decision, particularly in light of the many concerns that have surfaced in the Mumia Abu-Jamal case over apparent judicial bias during the trial itself.

THE FRATERNAL ORDER OF POLICE: LEADING THE CALL FOR THE EXECUTION OF MUMIA ABU-JAMAL

"If you don't like it you can join him [Abu-Jamal]. We'll take out the electric chair, we'll make it an electric couch. Our position on this will not brook any type of equivocation, any delay or anything else." Richard Costello, President of the Philadelphia Fraternal Order of Police.[37]

The Philadelphia Fraternal Order of Police (FOP) has continually campaigned for Abu-Jamal's execution.[38] The organization has also reacted with hostility to the many prominent people calling for a new trial for Abu-Jamal. In August 1999, the FOP's national biennial general meeting passed a resolution calling for an economic boycott of all individuals and businesses that had expressed support for freeing Abu-Jamal. A spokesman for the organization stated: "It is wrong to allow companies and individuals to profit from the murder of an officer who made the ultimate sacrifice by trying to protect and serve the citizens of his community. And we will not rest until Abu-Jamal burns in hell." The FOP has strong ties with the state judiciary that adjudicated Abu-Jamal's appeals (see below). In 1994, Pennsylvania State Representative Mike McGeehan was quoted as stating: "I want to see Mumia Abu-Jamal die. I don't care how many Hollywood types are for him, we're going to see him die in Pennsylvania."[39]

The administration of capital justice in the USA is highly politicised and support for the death penalty is seen by many politicians and judicial officials as popular with the electorate; significantly, most state court judges and prosecutors must run for election in order to obtain or retain their positions.[40] Where the judiciary is part of the political process, the support or opposition of the law enforcement community for candidates can significantly affect both the outcome of judicial elections and the decisions of elected officials in death penalty cases.

In Pennsylvania, the justices who serve on the state Supreme Court are elected to their positions. Given the politicized nature of the death penalty in the USA, Amnesty International remains concerned about the political support received by members of the Pennsylvania Supreme Court by a law enforcement community so vigorously committed to the execution of Mumia Abu-Jamal.[41]

The law enforcement community's support for some members of the Court is both prominent and extensive:

Chief Justice John P. Flaherty has been presented with a Justice Award by the Sheriff's Association of Pennsylvania; Justice Ralph J. Cappy (who wrote the opinion denying Abu-Jamal a new trial) has been awarded "Man of the Year" by Pennsylvania State Police and "Man of the Year" by Pennsylvania Fraternal Order of Police; Justice Ronald D. Castille has been awarded a "Distinguished Public Service Award" by the Pennsylvania County and State Detectives Association, a "Layman Award" by the Pennsylvania Chiefs of Police Association and "Man of the Year" by Fraternal Order of Police Lodge No. 5 (Philadelphia); Justice Sandra Schultz Newman was honoured by the Police Chiefs Association of Southeastern Pennsylvania for "dedicated leadership and outstanding contributions to the community and law enforcement."

Were any of the Court's members to vote to uphold Abu-Jamal's appeals, these strong affiliations with a highly-influential organization lobbying for Abu-Jamal's execution raises the probability that they would suffer a severe political backlash from the media and other politicians, thereby jeopardising their future on the bench.[42]

Mumia Abu-Jamal's appeals at state level are now exhausted, and his case has entered the federal courts. Under the terms of the *Anti-Terrorism and Effective Death Penalty Act* (AEDPA), which President Clinton signed into law in 1996, the federal appellate courts must defer to the findings of the state courts of appeal in all but the most exceptional circumstances.[43] It remains unclear whether the restrictions of the AEDPA apply broadly to cases tried prior to its enactment. The federal courts that are preparing to review Mumia Abu-Jamal's appeals may thus be bound by the suspect rulings of the lower courts, even when deciding on crucial issues that received cursory or unsatisfactory review at the state level.

The record in this case indicates a pattern of events that compromised Abu-Jamal's right to a fair trial, including irregularities in the police investigation and the prosecution's presentation of the case, the possible coercion or exclusion of key witnesses, the appearance of judicial bias and the state's failure to provide the means necessary for an adequate defence. Years of appellate review have failed to allay or address these fundamental concerns, nor is it certain that the federal courts will be empowered to grant relief.

UNDER SENTENCE OF DEATH: CONDITIONS ON PENNSYLVANIA'S DEATH ROW

The UN Economic and Social Council has urged states which retain the death penalty to "effectively apply the (UN) Standard Minimum Rules for the Treatment of Prisoners, in order to keep to a minimum the suffering of prisoners under sentence of death and to avoid any exacerbation of such suffering."[44]

In 1997, the Secretary General of Amnesty International, Pierre Sané, visited death rows in Texas and Pennsylvania. In both prisons he witnessed the appalling conditions and regimes inflicted on condemned inmates.[45]

In State Correctional Institution Greene (SCI Greene), the Secretary General met with death row inmates Mumia

Abu-Jamal and Scott Blystone. At a press conference following the visit, Pierre Sané described SCI Greene: "Death row in Pennsylvania looks and feels like a morgue. Everything is high-tech, and there is no human being in sight. From the moment that condemned prisoners arrive, the state tries to kill them slowly, mechanically and deliberately—first spiritually, and then physically."

Scott Blystone described to the delegation the intense strain of undergoing preparation for execution, a process both he and Abu-Jamal suffered in 1995:

"They [the guards] come to your cell, you know you're getting a [death] warrant because they're real polite. They handcuff you, belt you and shackle your feet. It's silent, you can hear your heart beating. They take you to death watch—cells surrounded by plexiglass walls so sound can't get through. There's a camera at the front of your cell that watches you 24-hours a day. You're standing there alive and they're asking you where to send your body. After surviving a death warrant I felt like I'd lost my soul—it kills part of you."

Both Mumia Abu-Jamal and Scott Blystone told the delegation about widespread and frequent brutality inflicted upon prisoners by prison guards in SCI Greene, a long-term concern of Amnesty International. In May 1998 four SCI Greene guards were fired from their jobs and at least a further 21 were demoted, suspended or reprimanded because of their treatment of inmates.

SCI Greene is in a predominately white rural area; 93 per cent of prison staff are white. However, the vast majority of the inmates are African Americans or Hispanics from urban areas, leading to high levels of racial tension and allegations of racial abuse. A newspaper article written following the sacking of the guards, quoting from both guards and prisoners, detailed regular occurrences of racism and violence by prison workers.[46] The allegations included guards beating prisoners and then writing KKK (i.e. Ku Klux Klan) with the inmates blood; the "working over" (beating) of certain prisoners by guards upon the instruction of superior officers to "adjust their attitudes"; and guards spitting tobacco juice into inmates' food.

Despite assurances received from the Pennsylvania Department of Corrections (in a reply to a letter concerning the abuse of women prisoners on death row in

---

**SCI GREENE PRISON AUTHORITIES:
VIOLATING ABU-JAMAL'S RIGHT TO SECURE
COMMUNICATIONS WITH HIS LEGAL TEAM.**

All US prisoners have the right to exchange information with their legal representatives in confidentiality. In 1995, prison authorities admitted they had copied privileged mail sent by attorneys to Abu-Jamal, on the grounds that they were investigating a rule violation by him. In 1996, a district court ruled that such acts "actually injured" Abu-Jamal and were in violation of his Constitutional rights under the Sixth and Fourteenth Amendments.

This right is also protected under Principle 8 of the UN's Basic Principles on the Roles of Lawyers.

SCI Muncy) that prison guards act in a professional manner towards condemned inmates, Amnesty International continues to receive complaints from prisoners. For example, in September 1999, the organization received detailed allegations of racist abuse directed at condemned prisoners in SCI Greene, including accounts of prisoners refusing to eat food served by the guards on a specific shift who were placing "non food" items in meals.

On 13 October 1999, Governor Ridge of Pennsylvania signed a death warrant ordering Abu-Jamal's execution on 2 December 1999. Amnesty International believes the execution order was signed solely for political reasons as the governor would have been aware that Abu-Jamal was to file an appeal within the next two weeks that would automatically stayed the execution. In a statement, Amnesty International drew a comparison between the governor's act and the act of torture: "This death warrant serves no purpose except to put Mumia Abu-Jamal on 'death watch'—causing him unnecessary suffering. This is playing politics with a man's life. The unnecessary infliction of suffering upon a prisoner by a government official constitutes torture."

CONCLUSION

Capital punishment may only be carried out pursuant to a final judgement rendered by a competent court after a legal process which gives all possible safeguards to ensure a fair trial, at least equal to those contained in article 14 of the International Covenant on Civil and Political Rights..."[47]

For the diminishing list of countries which still resort to the death penalty, international human rights standards require the very highest level of fairness in capital cases, given the irreversible nature of the penalty.

The trial of Mumia Abu-Jamal took place in an atmosphere of animosity and tension, much of it directed against the defendant. As the judge at the first pretrial hearing stated: "I know there are certain cases that have explosive tendencies in this community, and this is one of them." That animosity has endured throughout the 17 years since the trial, particularly within the law enforcement community. In 1995, upon learning of Mumia Abu-Jamal's stay of execution, Philadelphia police officer James Green said: "It makes you wonder. Maybe we should have executed him at 13th and Locust [the crime scene] where he executed Danny Faulkner."[48]

The law enforcement community's unseemly agitation for the execution of Mumia Abu-Jamal is just one of Amnesty International's concerns over this case.

Many of the deficiencies that Amnesty International has identified in the Mumia Abu-Jamal case mirror broader concerns over the application of the death penalty nationwide. Concern about possible judicial bias is not limited to Pennsylvania and the resources provided to indigent defendants are pitifully inadequate in many jurisdictions. Police misconduct has been cited in many cases and the risk of wrongful convictions in capital trials remains alarmingly high.[49]

Amnesty International remains concerned that the relationship between the Pennsylvania judiciary and the law enforcement community at the very least gives rise to the unfortunate impression that justice is a one-way street leading to Mumia Abu-Jamal's eventual execution. The Pennsylvania Supreme Court, for example, appears to have ignored its own previous precedents in denying the defendant's appeals.

Proponents of the execution of Abu-Jamal maintain that he had a "fair" trial and was duly convicted and sentenced by a jury of his peers. The adversarial system of justice in the USA can only be a fair arbiter if the defence and prosecution have reasonable access to the resources necessary to present their version of events, and if the judge overseeing the case is truly neutral. Juries can only be accurate assessors of events if they are given a complete view of the facts—including any differing explanations and interpretations of events—and are made aware of the possible reasons for the bias of witnesses. These factors were clearly missing in Abu-Jamal's trial.

During the trial of Mumia Abu-Jamal, the jury was left unaware of much of the crucial information regarding the death of Officer Faulkner.

Other factors present during the prosecution of this case also render the verdict and sentence fundamentally unsound, including inadequate trial representation, the overt hostility of the trial judge and the appearance of judicial bias during appellate review.

Based on its review of the trial transcript and other original documents, Amnesty International has determined that numerous aspects of this case clearly failed to meet minimum international standards safeguarding the fairness of legal proceedings. Amnesty International therefore believes that the interests of justice would best be served by the granting of a new trial to Mumia Abu-Jamal. The trial should fully comply with international standards of justice and should not allow for the reimposition of the death penalty. The organization is also recommending that the retrial take place in a neutral venue, where the case has not polarized the public as it has in Philadelphia. Finally, the authorities should permit prominent jurists from outside the USA to observe the proceedings, to ensure that the retrial complies in all respects with universally-recognized human rights safeguards.

NOTES

1 For further information see *Rights for All*, AI index AMR 51/35/98, ISBN 0 86210 274 X, published October 1998.

2 For example, in 1995, six Philadelphia police officers pleaded guilty to charges of planting illegal drugs on suspects, the theft of more than $100,000 and the falsification of reports. The investigations into the officers actions have led to the release of hundreds of defendants whose convictions were overturned by the appeal courts. Also in 1995, two other officers from Philadelphia received prison sentences of five to 10 years for framing young men. Since 1993, the city of Philadelphia has paid out approximately $27 million in more than 230 lawsuits alleging police misconduct.

3 *Above the Law: Police and Excessive Use of Force*, Jerome H. Skolnick and James J. Fyfe, published by The Free Press.

4 *Frank Rizzo: The Last Big Man in Big City America*, S.A. Paolantonio, pubished by Camino Books.

5 The MOVE organization formed in Philadelphia during the early 1970s. The group follows the teaching of John Africa. Its manifesto includes: "MOVE work is to stop industry from poisoning the air...and to put an end to the enslavement of life...the purpose of John Africa's revolution is to show people how corrupt, rotten, criminally enslaving this system is...and to set the example of revolution for people to follow when they realize how they've been oppressed, repressed, duped, tricked by this system, this government and see the need to rid themselves of this cancerous system as MOVE does." (Description taken from "25 Years on the MOVE," published by MOVE.)

6 A similar incident occurred in 1985, when a stand-off developed between police and members of MOVE. The siege was ended when a police helicopter dropped an incendiary device on the house, killing 11 of its occupants, including six children (only two occupants survived). The device also started a fire that destroyed over

60 houses in the predominately black area. In 1995, a federal jury awarded MOVE members $1.5 million after determining that the city of Philadelphia had violated their constitutional right to protection against unreasonable search and seizure when the police dropped the bomb.

7   Amnesty International has long-term concerns around COIN-TELPRO. In 1981, the organization called for a commission of inquiry into FBI operations which it believed had undermined the fairness of trials involving several BPP members and members of the American Indian Movement. Amnesty International also called for a retrial for Geronimo ji Jaga Pratt when evidence came to light after his trial that he had been targeted for "neutralization" by COINTELPRO. Pratt was released from prison in 1998 after 27 years in prison after his conviction was overturned on appeal because of new evidence showing that the key prosecution's witness was a police informer (which he had denied while testifying).

8   *Philadelphia Inquirer,* 10 December 1981.

9   Principle 2 of the Basic Principles on the Independence of the Judiciary. Adopted by the Seventh United Nations Congress on the Prevention of Crime and the Treatment of Offenders held at Milan from 26 August to 6 September 1985 and endorsed by General assembly resolutions 40/32 of 29 November 1985 and 40/146 of 13 December 1985.

10 See page 28 for more information regarding the Fraternal Order of Police.

11 Of the 124 prisoners from Philadelphia on death row in October 1998, only 15 were white. Studies of the administration of the death penalty in the USA have consistently found evidence that race of defendant and/or victim can play a major role in who is sentenced to die. One such study found that, even after making allowances for case differences, blacks in Philadelphia were substantially more likely to receive death sentences than other defendants who committed similar murders (D. Baldus, et al., *Race Discrimination and the Death Penalty in the Post Furman Era: An Empirical and Legal Overview, with Preliminary Findings from Philadelphia*, Cornell Law Review, Volume 83, September 1998.).

12 *What price justice?: Poor defendants pay the cost as courts save money on murder trials,* published 13 September 1992.

13 *Guilty and Framed,* Stuart Taylor, Jr. *The American Lawyer,* published December 1995.

14 Principle 13 of the Basic Principles on the Role of Lawyers, adopted by consensus at the Eighth United Nations Congress on the Prevention of Crime and the Treatment of Offenders in 1990 and welcomed by the UN General Assembly.

15 For example, George McFarland was tried and sentenced to death in Texas in 1991. At trial he was represented by a lawyer who continually fell asleep during the proceedings. When asked about the lawyer sleeping, the trial judge explained that this did not violate McFarland's Constitutional right to be represented because "the Constitution does not say the lawyer has to be awake." For further information see *Is Fairness Irrelevant? The Evisceration of Federal Habeas Corpus Review and Limits on the Ability of State Courts to Protect Fundamental Rights,* Stephen B. Bright *Washington and Lee Law Review,* Vol. 54, No. 1 (Winter 1997).

16 International Commission of Jurists: *Administration of the death penalty in the United States. Report of a Mission.* June 1996. For more information see *USA: A macabre assembly line of death: Death penalty developments in 1997.* AI index AMR 51/20/98, published April 1998.

17 Comments of the HRC: USA, UN Doc. CCPR/C/79/Add.50 , 7 April 1995, para. 23. The ICCPR was signed by the USA on 5 October 1977 and ratified on 8 June 1992. In 1997, the UN Special Rapporteur on extrajudicial, summary and arbitrary executions also stated that the "lack of adequate counsel and legal representation for many capital defendants is disturbing" following his visit to the USA in 1997. UN Doc E/CN.4/1998/68/Add.3

18 Despite the subsequent introduction of competency standards for appointed counsel, the administration of the death penalty in Pennsylvania continues to be a major concern to Amnesty International and other organizations. In 1997, the Philadelphia Bar Association passed a resolution calling for a general moratorium on the use of the death penalty. The resolution cited the "substantial risk that

the death penalty continues to be imposed in an arbitrary, capricious and discriminatory manner" and called upon the moratorium to continue until "such time as the fair and impartial administration of the death penalty can be ensured and the risk that innocent persons may be executed is minimized."

19 Article 14(3)(d) of the International Covenant on Civil and Political Rights, ratified by the USA in 1992 states: "*In the determination of any criminal charges against him, everyone shall be entitled to the following minimum guarantees, in full equality:... (d)To be tried in his presence, and to defend himself in person or through legal assistance of his own choosing...*"

20 John Africa had successfully represented himself against federal charges of illegal ownership of weapons in 1981.

21 Judge Sabo also sanctioned lawyers representing Abu-Jamal in the 1995 hearing, fining one and temporarily imprisoning another. It is extremely rare for judges to sanction lawyers in the USA.

22 Article 8 (2) (f) of the American Convention on Human Rights. The USA signed the Convention but has yet to ratify it.

23 Numerous other states, such as California, provide two attorneys in death penalty cases. The American Bar Association's "Guidelines for the Appointment and Performance of Counsel in Death Penalty Cases" specifies "In cases where the death penalty is sought, two qualified attorneys should be assigned to represent the defendant."

24 Pretrial hearing on 1 April 1982. A calendar judge sets the schedule for the trial and oversees the granting of funds to the defence attorneys for experts, etc.

25 Amnesty International has recorded many instances of the pitifully inadequate resources afforded by the state to capital defendants across the USA. The funding provided by the city of Philadelphia for legitimate defence expenses in capital cases is particularly deficient. In 1992, the Death Penalty Information Center (DPIC), published *Justice on the Cheap: The Philadelphia Story.* The report detailed many examples of inadequate defence funding in capital trials in Philadelphia, concluding that "any pretense to equal justice is fatally undermined" and that "justice is becoming ever more

just another commodity available only to the few who can afford it." The report is available from DPIC, 1320 Eighteenth Street, NW, Washington DC, USA or via website www.essential.org/dpic

26 Alternate jurors are to be used in the event that a member of the jury is unable to take part in the deliberations because of illness, misconduct, etc.

27 *Batson v Kentucky.* For further information see *Killing with Prejudice: Race and the Death Penalty in the USA* (page 12), AI index AMR 51/52/99, published May 1999.

28 The jury was 'sequestered' during the trial (housed in a hotel and forbidden contact with the outside world).

29 Dissenting in the case of Mexican national Cesar Fierro.

30 Officer Bell was Daniel Faulkner's police partner and "best friend." Priscilla Durham, who at first denied knowing Faulkner, later admitted that she had spoken to him on several occasions, sometimes over coffee.

31 Abu-Jamal's allegation that he was severely beaten by police has not been upheld. However, several police officers admitted during their trial testimony that they "accidentally" hit Abu-Jamal's head against a pole and dropped him on his face while carrying him to the police wagon.

32 The appeal brief can be found at:
http://mojo.calyx.net/~refuse/mumia/101699petition.html

33 Article 26 of the ICCPR.

34 The trial transcript for the sentencing hearing can be found on internet at: http://mojo.calyx.net/~refuse/mumia/082599july3trans.html

35 Sworn affidavit of former State Representative David P. Richardson, dated May 1995.

36 The Supreme Court also ruled that: "the Commonwealth can only present evidence as to the aggravating circumstances set out in the [death penalty] statue" in the case of *Commonwealth v Holcomb* in 1985. The aggravating circumstances in the statue to not include a defendant's political views or comments.

37 Transcript of Channel 10 (WCAU) interview, 14 July 1990.

38 The Fraternal Order of Police is the nation's largest organization of law enforcement professionals, with more than 283,000 members.

39 Quoted in *The Philadelphia Daily News*, 2 June 1994.

40 Also see *Judges and the Politics of Death: Deciding Between the Bill of Rights and the Next Election in Capital Cases*, by Stephen B. Bright and Patrick J. Keenan (*Boston University Law Review*, Volume 75, Number 3 May 1995). Also available via website: http://www.schr.org/reports/index.html

41 "The [UN Human Rights] Committee is concerned about the impact which the current system of election of judges may, in a few States, have on the implementation of the rights provided under article 14 of the [International] Covenant [on Civil and Political Rights] and welcomes the efforts of a number os States in the adoption of a selection system based on merit...." "The Committee recommends that the current system in a few States of appointment of judges through elections be reconsidered with a view to its replacement by a system of appointment on merit by an independent body." Comments of the Human Rights Committee. CCPR/C/79/Add.50. Paragraphs 23 and 36.

42 Amnesty International has documented numerous occasions where judges were criticized, and sometimes removed from office by the electorate, for upholding the appeal of a condemned inmate. For example, Penny White was removed by the electorate from her position on the Tennessee Supreme Court after being attacked for her ruling overturning the death sentence of Richard Odom. For further information see *USA: Death penalty developments in 1996*, AI index AMR 51/01/97. In October 1999, the US Senate rejected President Clinton's nomination of Ronnie White for the position of federal district judge. The Republican Senators all voted against White, citing what they perceived as his reluctance to vote to uphold death sentences. One Senator said: "During his tenure [on the Missouri Supreme Court], he has far more frequently dissented in capital cases than any other judge." (*Los Angeles Times*, 5 October 1999).

43 For more details on the Act please see *USA: Death penalty developments in 1996*, AI index AMR 51/01/97, published March 1997.

44 ECOSOC Resolution 1996/15, adopted on 23 July 1996.

45 For details for the Secretary General's visit to Texas death row please see *Lethal Injustice: the Death Penalty in Texas*, AI index AMR 51/10/98, published March 1998.

46 "Firings and charges have shaken up SCI Greene," *Pittsburgh Post-Gazette*, 11 August 1998.

47 Paragraph 5, Safeguards guaranteeing protection of the rights of those facing the death penalty, adopted by the UN Economic and Social Council in resolution 1984/50 on 25 May 1984 and endorsed by the UN General Assembly in resolution 39/118, adopted without a vote on 14 December 1984.

48 Quoted in the *New York Times* on 8 August 1995. Amnesty International is appalled that a police officer would openly espouse the possibility of an extrajudicial execution.

49 Further documentation of these allegations can be found in the numerous Amnesty International publications listed on the inside cover of this

AMNESTY INTERNATIONAL is a worldwide campaigning movement that works to promote all the human rights enshrined in the Universal Declaration of Human Rights and other international standards. In particular, Amnesty International campaigns to free all prisoners of conscience; ensure fair and prompt trials for political prisoners; abolish the death penalty, torture and other cruel treatment of prisoners; end political killings and "disappearances"; and oppose human rights abuses by opposition groups.

Amnesty International USA
322 Eighth Avenue
NY, NY 10001
http://www.amnestyusa.org